Unsung Hero Reveals the Truth of Propaganda and Mixed Messages

Author Vickie Boyle

Co-Author Carolynn Boyle

Acknowledgment

I would like to express my gratitude and support to my family, friends and publishers Tyler and April have been tremendous support getting this manuscript to print with Ingram sparks. Aneurysm Awareness and Intervention Saves Lives. It has been a struggle for me at times however family like my granddaughter co-author Carolynn Boyle has been my life line and tremendous support to drop another Bucket List to do with Grace of God. We Did It.

Contents

Foreword

The awaking Truth of Mixed Messages from our political Leaders can be devastating, with false propaganda and fear of Adolf Hitler's ideology of the Super Race.

People were fooled. German language students I met, told me WWII never happened.

Getting this book translated from German to English took fifty years. It is written to tell the history of how the Nazi regime came to power. The manuscript of my literary collection of war relics, letters, memoirs and photographs tells the story of the Social Science and political uprising during WWII in its Raw beginning. Propaganda perfectionist Dr. Joseph Gobbles took media publication to the masses of people to win the support of the German people who indoctrinated the ideology of Adolf Hitler.

History repeats itself like World Wars and Civil Wars, it is surreal when you recognize it. Like now!

Unsung Hero reveals the Truth of propaganda and "Mixed Messages"

It is my pleasure and honor to join authorship with my granddaughter Carolynn. She's a brilliant young woman 2024 Graduate with a 4.4 GPA Cambridge Honor Student. She can bring the new generation to the history lesson of WWII and how History Repeats itself.

Local WWII veterans, former residents of Putnam County Florida reveal the Truth of how the Holocaust happened, how the German SS soldiers exterminated thousands of Jews and others who opposed the Super Race indoctrination.

Stopping the violence and hate for the sake of world peace begins with an understanding of what happened and how the Holocaust happened. With many Holocaust museums displaying massive collections of evidence of its victimization, torture and death were devastating beyond measure.

My father-in-law, Sgt Hawley Boyle and life-long family friend, Captain Mary K Ried ARN, left behind their experiences of stories they witnessed and wanted to be commentators of the Truth. I'm proud to have known them and it's my honor and duty to express my gratitude to bring this story on their behalf. They wanted to teach the history of what they experienced to end the war of all wars. WWII.

As mentioned in my short story paperback book "1st Lt Mary K Reid," her memoirs told the horror stories their patients told the Concentration Camp Liberators. The Allied Forces ordered all Nazi publications to be destroyed.

Sgt. Hawley j Boyle said the Nazi books he brought back from Germany told a story of how a nation was fooled by the propaganda publication of Dr Joseph Gobbles.

Thirteen volumes distributed throughout grocery stores like collecting Green Stamps was a clever way to spread their political stance on taking over the world. Ruling a Super Nation of perfect people perfect World. A Super Race.

He wanted the literary material in social science conversations of awareness WWII, in fact, happened, when the world revealed the truth about the Holocaust, Concentration Camps and the spread of racial Hate.

Putnam county Florida

Our local unsung heroes remain in remembrance with gratitude.

- At eas Sir,

- Sgt. Hawley Boyle

- At eas Ma'am

- Captain Mary K Reid

Your stories have been told.

Sergeant Hawley Boyle

From basic training as a US Army private to being US Army Sgt. Hawley Boyle. Lake Forrest College Illinois, who graduate deployed to Germany for duty as General Clerk of hospital publications.

He was the most non-violent person on earth, a gentle giant. He felt a duty to serve in the military to do his part to end the war of all wars WWII.

He loved playing baseball in college and played on a semi-pro team. So when asked to play on APO 171 US ARMY 1st. Constabulary Regiment team, he was so happy to play and write home about it to his wife.

He received a commendation letter from General Harmon, on September 27, 1946, from Colonel Edward Maloney. 1st Constabulary Regiment for being the winning baseball team.

He sent letters home to his wife about the games and never talked about the horrors of war he saw in the aftermath of Hitler's devastating destruction of the Third Reich.

Sgt. Boyle was General Clerk with US Army 386th Station Hospital, he was in charge of publications and supervised ten other Clerks making up and issuing hospital publications.

Watching the burning books in the street of the propaganda publication by Dr. Joseph Gobbles to demolish the core of the Nazi regime was surreal.

The sights and smells of war were still in the air. The horror stories he heard about and the ruins of so many cities bombed to pieces remained in his memory.

He recognized an association of How the Native American Indian's demise on the Trail of Tears was admired by Adolf Hitler.

Like the box car train ride of prisoners that ended their lives as they got to Concentration Camps to gas chambers, using prisoners as slaves for various jobs. Medical experiments, family separation, starvation, diseases and being murdered.

He sincerely apologized to me for the US government doing the same to my people, Native Americans. It was the first time I ever heard anyone admitting the wrong that was done to the American Indian.

Kill the Indian and civilize the Indian children like at Carlisle Boarding School at Pine Ridge Reservation.

As mentioned in my previous book, Adolf Hitler.

It's fitting my granddaughter Carolynn Boyle, co-author, his great-granddaughter is picking up the torch of his legacy to teach about the history of social science and it is repeating itself if we don't learn from what is Revealed from the Heroes that fought for the World's freedom.

God Bless America and the Allied Forces of WWII.

Chapter 1

The Führer as Speaker

By

Dr. Joseph Goebbels

November 1934 in Munich. The Fibrer seats in front of the Fehermhälle to the members of the Youth and the League of German Girls who have been newly admitted into the party

There are two kinds of speakers, which differ fundamentally and essentially from one another: those who speak from the mind and those who speak from the heart. Accordingly, they also address two kinds of people: those who speak from the mind and those who receive from the heart. Parliament generally produces speakers who speak from the mind; the people produce speakers who speak from the heart.

The speaker, from the mind, if he wants to speak effectively, must have sovereignty over a large material of state tics and knowledge. He must master dialectics like a pianist masters the keyboard. With the icy coldness of a relentlessly developing logic, he assembles his series of ideas and draws from them fine, inescapable conclusions. He works mainly on people who work primarily or exclusively with their intellect. He is not able to achieve great and thrilling successes. He does not know how to stir the masses to their core and warm them up to great, heaven-reaching goals. He sticks to the purely didactic.

At that time, they had always tried to deceive, on the one hand, by turning a triumphant event into disgraceful news in their newspapers. But then they got their hands on it, and this is where the whole debacle began. All the prosecutors and those who wanted to lead the accused or witnesses, including Hitler, astray with merciless, irritating questions or stupid, shimmering remarks were aware of this relentless, ruthless offensive. The People's Court trial of 1924 sought to legally settle the uprising of 9 November 1923. It was a triumphant victory for the accused because the Führer countered the mountains of documents, nonsense, and incomprehension with the radiant power of his open truthfulness and the striking effect of his eloquence. The Republic may not have taken note of the outcome of the Leipzig Reichswehr trial without regret, which was intended to destroy the Führer and his movement, but in reality, it became a springboard for his oratorical effectiveness that spread throughout the world.

Today, one remembers with horror the fact that a Jewish communist lawyer was allowed to put him to the test before a Berlin court for hours without a break in front of a rapid fire of questions and notes. One can take pride in the fact that Jewish Bolshevism was faced with an opponent who relentlessly attacked it with words and ideas, without giving up until it was overwhelmed. We saw and experienced the Führer as a speaker at the parade for Freedom Day in 1935. He spoke to the crowd fifteen times over seven days. Not once did the same thought or phrase reappear. Everything seemed fresh, young, vital, and forceful. He spoke differently to the officials than he did to the SA and SS men, and differently to the youth than to the women.

But he was at his greatest as a speaker when addressing smaller circles. He turned to them in eternal change, speaking to each individual listener, creating a personal connection. His conversation had a moving flow that instantly captured attention and kept the listeners engaged because each one felt personally addressed. He discussed topics with expert knowledge, astonishing everyone and leaving even the specialists in awe. Everyday topics suddenly gained universal significance in his words.

In smaller gatherings, he delved more intimately and deeply than public speeches allowed, reaching the core of issues and exposing them with relentless logic. Only those who have heard him speak in this way can fully appreciate the extent of his oratorical genius. His speeches to the people and the world are words that resonate in a way history has rarely seen, and they leave a lasting impact on the formation of a new international era.

There is hardly a person in the entire civilized world today who has not at least heard the sound of his voice, and whether they understood his words or not, they have been touched by the magic of his tone in their innermost being. Our people can count themselves fortunate to know that they have a voice above them that the world listens to, a voice that shapes thoughts into words and moves an era into action. This man is one of those rare individuals with the courage to say "yes" and "no" without distorting it with an "if" or "but." In a time when millions and millions across all countries are suffering from the greatest tribulations and terrible distress, when hardly a star can be seen in the dark clouds overshadowing Europe, and when the peoples are driven by dull longings they cannot express, he stands above Germany as one of the countless millions who, when man falls silent in his torment, has been given by God the ability to say what we are all suffering.

The Führer speaks to the German People

The subtle quake comes, rising with a tone that Beffer knows well, reverberating over the so-called vines of the most brilliant minds. Once again, the burden is felt, promoting our national rebirth from the central banks. He has a number of formulations at his disposal. This time, the listener feels that something significant has just been said. Time and again, the same great, sustaining principles of our national rebirth are hammered home in ever-changing forms. This style of oratory lacks any rigid doctrinaire element. If a fact is presented as an assertion, it appears throughout the course of the speech to be supported by an inexhaustible wealth of examples. These examples are not drawn from the life and society of just one class, but from the life of the entire people, so that all classes find their own foundation in them. They are delivered with such a strength of feeling that even the most blindly enraged opponent eventually capitulates, recognizing that this speaker, unlike all parliamentary jugglers, believes what he says. He brings everyday life to vivid life.

In his speeches to the youth, the damage of time is not dealt with through trade but with a blend of wisdom and caustic wit. Humor triumphs here—crying with one eye and laughing with the other. The worries and troubles of daily life are unmistakably heard. A key sign of a successful speech is whether it reads well on paper, not just sounds good. The Führer's speeches are stylistic masterpieces, whether he improvises off the cuff, develops them from a few scattered keywords, or reads them from a meticulously crafted concept at important international events. Those who are not in his immediate presence could hardly tell whether the written speech that is read aloud was delivered freely or if the freely delivered speech was written in advance. Both are powerful tools of persuasion. The Reich Party Rally of 1935 exemplifies speeches that are ready for print in the best sense of the word.

This picture would not be complete without giving sufficient mention to the Führer as an outstanding designer and master of oratory. The last time the general public had the opportunity to witness him in such a role was in a memorable confrontation with the Social Democrats in the Reichstag in 1933, when he responded to a clumsy and impudent jeremiad by then-Reichstag deputy Wels. It felt like a game of nonsense was being played, with Marxism driven from one corner to another. And wherever it hoped for mercy, it found only destruction. The oratorical blows fell with breathtaking precision. Without a transcript, without notes, the Führer met face-to-face with those Social Democratic parliamentary veterans, who were receiving their final blow. How often had he referenced them in his speeches over the years?

Before the Youth

RReich Party Rally of 1935

Vickie Boyle & Carolynn Boyle

The Führer in the election campaign for Germany's freedom in March 1936

In all ages, at large theaters, small concerts, and brute-force concerts, there were more crises than ever before. When Bery could conquer the palace, boxing was in a time of its own. When Bismarck stood in rebuke, he played a significant role in the cold storm. The collapse of the World War gave rise to a new, powerful Bohemian fleet. What the bastions won in this case was small, but it was sufficient for domestic use, in the parliament or for the supervisory

8

board. However, in the final vote, it only flowed into the reserves. This was likely due to the times themselves—they had no great ambitions or sky-high projects but were drowning in a dull feeling of satiation. The only apparent defense against them was Marxism, which was allied with the majority and represented a form of filialism that could never ignite the spark of true genius.

But revolutions give birth to true speakers, and revolutions are made by true speakers! In their course, one must not overlook the written or printed word. However, the spoken word ignites with the secret magic of its immediate effect.

Thus acted over the centuries as the eternal heralds of great contemporary ideas that made history and shaped the lives of nations. It also seems as if the Basques were endowed with different talents, as if there were people who were too shy for this stirring art and others who were predestined for it. It is not for nothing that we speak of Latin eloquence. The great abundance of mediocre and significant rhetorical talents, particularly in Romance peoples, gives this term a certain legitimacy. And it is probably in the spirit of this fact that talents for oratory here also find an audience that understands them, supports them and gives them the widest possible scope for impact.

Our German people have been in a bad position in this regard throughout the past. They have produced statesmen and soldiers, philosophers and scientists, musicians and poets. Builders and engineers, plan.

It is perceived with the eyes and ears, and the sweeping force of the masses, who are moved by the sound of a human voice, irresistibly captivates even those who are still wavering and doubting. Where would be the statesmanlike genius that could achieve a higher? It would have been impossible for the inscrutable fate to have placed itself in the shadows of life from the very beginning, if it had not had the power of speech and the explosive power of the word at its disposal! It gives it the opportunity to turn all dreams and ideas into realities. With its help, it gathers people around its flag who are determined to fight for it; driven by it, men risk their health and lives in order to lead a new world to victory. The organization is formed from the propaganda of the word, the movement develops from the organization, and the movement conquers the state. It is not just a matter of getting ideas right.

Speech to the Workforce at Blohm & Vob

Takeover of the Reichsfuhrerschule in 1933

Winter holidays in the mountains with Ben Langen's men's band, Bitter Columbus. My greetings come to a close. No other leader in this country, aside from Beecher, possesses such a genius for mass production that is both strange and unique. He has never been before and is not one to be suspected of needing stardom or even a magnificent house. He acts entirely on his own, without help from anyone else, perhaps even deliberately. I cannot imagine that the Führer would ever have spoken differently than he did the first time. He says what comes directly from his mind, and that is why he connects so deeply with his audience.

He has a wonderful ability to sense what is in the air with his intuition. He expresses it so clearly, literally, and without reservation that the audience is led to believe that it was not just his perspective being presented—it feels as if it was always their own thoughts. That is the real secret behind the magical effect of Hitler's speech. The Führer is neither purely a speaker of reason nor of poetry. He speaks from both as the situation demands.

The most important traits of his addresses to the people are clarity of structure, relentlessness in the logical development of a series of thoughts, simplicity, and general intelligibility. His speech is marked by razor-sharp dialectics, a keen and never-misleading instinct for the people's feelings, a restrained use of pathos, and a call to the soul that never goes unanswered by the people.

The Führer once spoke, four years ago, when he was still far from power, at a meeting attended mostly by political opponents. Initially, he met with icy rejection. In a two-hour speech, there was something essential—he managed to expose all the pretenses present at the time and, in front of the audience, he stripped away their orders and their authority. He spoke meter by meter, unmasking them and making his demands clear, addressing the time and the needs of the people. It was as though he wrestled with an opponent.

The Führer opened the 1935 Freedom Party Congress in the historic town hall in Nuremberg.

Often, yes, old Berntalle, he can bring in Menthen, but he can never mobilize them under Dintan Treung's tree. Mallen and a large distribution—very even with the acceptance of Ben Gettale and off at the calculator—were not asked, and he did not report on the man's side. It was not about the skills, but about mentality over permanence, over morphology. He knows how to expose and touch them with a chiseled hand, bringing ideas to life in works of broad declamation.

He captures people and their lands with his voice, a voice that rises melodiously above his audience, towering like pillars over his world. His voice, coming from the depths of the blood, evokes pride and stirs listeners to their very core. His melodious songs about human life bring salvation. He shakes up the lazy and complacent, lifts the lukewarm and timid, and makes the cowards learn and the weak triumph. History rarely hears such sounds. But when these voices penetrate a sluggish century with their omnipotence, peoples and conditions under them are profoundly shaped.

These rhetorical geniuses are the drumbeaters of fate. They are often lone individuals confronted with the crumbling epochs of history, suddenly and unexpectedly illuminated by the brightest spotlight of a new era. These are speakers who, like every great orator, have their own style. They can only speak as they are. Their words are tailor-made for them, whether in their appearance, posters, letters, or speeches—they speak the language that fits their nature.

History offers many examples that show how great speakers, though alike in the magnitude of their impact, appeal to the people in different ways. The Führer, with Reich Labor Leader Hierl, spoke in front of 47,000 workers at the Reich Party Congress in 1935 as a master of intellectual oratory. While many are gifted with artistic ability, which they use as true virtuosos of the poetic art, beyond that, the Führer has abilities hidden from most intellectual speakers. His clarity of diction is combined with a seemingly natural simplicity in expressing his thoughts. He instinctively knows what must be said and how to say it.

The greatness of his poetic vision is united with the monumental. His appeal to hearts varies according to the time, nation, and character of the era. Caesar spoke differently to his legions than Frederick the Great spoke to his grenadiers, just as Napoleon addressed his guards differently than Bismarck spoke to the representatives of the Prussian Landtag. Yet, each of them used language that resonated with the people before them, igniting their senses and finding echoes in their hearts. They gave vivid expression to the deepest and most mysterious forces of their time.

The Führer, with Reich Labor Leader Hierl, spoke in front of 47,000 workers at the Reich Party Congress in 1935

Chapter 2

The Führer in his Private Life

By

Obergruppenführer Wilhelm Brückner

Walk on the Obersalzberg

It is obvious that a man as absorbed in political work as the Führer must sacrifice his private life for it. When he tries to escape from the pressures of official business, political issues follow him to the farthest corners of the German homeland—whether to a small, quiet village on the Baltic Sea or to Haus Wachenfeld on the Obersalzberg. They pursue him not only through telephone calls, telegrams, letters, and documents but also through the constant presence of political concerns in his heart.

The concern for Germany is ever-present for the Führer; he goes to bed late at night with it, and he awakens early in the morning with it. He is beset by challenges in foreign policy, the demands of the new labor battle, issues in financial policy, the need to secure the food supply for the German people, matters of youth security, questions about German culture, and decisions concerning the restoration of German military security, and so, it goes on.

Despite everything, there is no experience that has not immediately brought him into the midst of the most important political questions, no experience that has not immediately reminded him of significant decisions. Everything in Germany begins with this man and ends with him. And if he seems to be relaxing for a few days, it is only preparation for new major decisions, for a new period of intense work. Even on a plane, he receives radio telegrams from his Reich leaders and ministers.

The Führer's private life has thus been absorbed into his public office and his work for the country. To speak of his private life is really only to say that it consists of moving his political work from the official rooms of the Reich Chancellery to less formal surroundings. Despite this, he still finds time to engage with all questions of art and science. He finds his greatest and most beautiful respite from the stress of daily work in music, whether in listening to an opera or a symphony concert. Only then is he completely detached from the burdens of the day, and many a great creative thought arises from his immersion in the vast realm of sounds.

At his official residence in the Reich Chancellery, he occasionally hosts leading German artists who share with him the finest creations of the time. After these artistic performances, discussions often continue late into the night on subjects such as music, drama, poetry, novels, architecture, and philosophy. Few leave such evenings without having gained valuable insights.

In addition to music, theater, and architecture, film, as the newest branch of artistic creation, particularly captures Führer's interest. A film projector is available to him on the Obersalzberg.

At the Obersalzberg, a neighbor greets the Führer

He is allowed to look through the telescope

Prime Minister Going with the Führer on the Obersalzberg.

The great advantage of the circle at the Führer's table is that he can discuss in more detail any topic that has particularly caught his attention during official lectures. This is why people from the most varied fields of work—officers and scientists, businessmen and artists, party leaders and veterans from the early days of the movement—often gather at his table. In these gatherings, they not only gain knowledge and inspiration but also enjoy enriching conversations with one another.

The Führer likes to use the weekends to personally gauge the mood of the people and assess the progress of reconstruction work without official announcements. He drives through various regions of Germany in the car he grew fond of during the struggle, and nearly every place he visits brings memories from that time to life. For his companions, witnessing the profound love the people show the Führer on these trips is always a deeply moving experience.

There are a few places in Germany to which the Führer frequently returns for relaxation. Chief among them is the house on the Obersalzberg, well known to all Germans and closely tied to the history of the movement. There are also houses on the Baltic and North Seas and a few secluded spots in the dunes that the Führer enjoys for a brief rest or for holding particularly important meetings.

A comrade from the field visits the Führer

Haus Wachenfeld on the Osbersalzberg near Berchtesgaden

Encounter at Obersalzberg

Walk in the Mountains

Days of rest. The Führer and little Helga Goebbels

Stew, also at the Reich Chancellor's

Good News

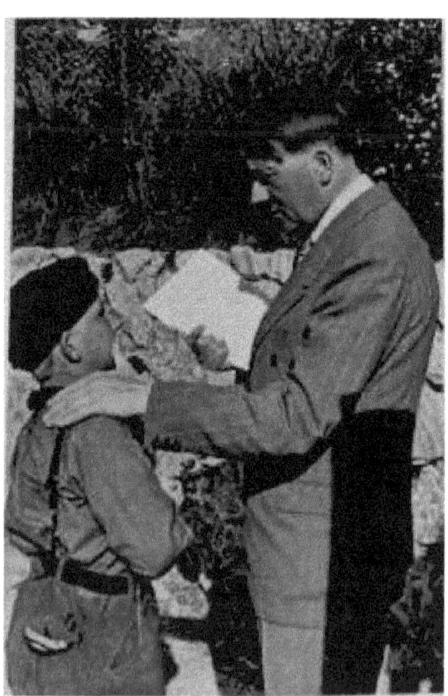

A boy hands the Führer a letter from his sick mother

A short visit to the guide on the Obersalzberg

Chapter 3

The Führer as Statesman

By

Dr. Joseph Goebbels

New year's Reception of the diplomatic corps in 1934

All human greatness has its origin in blood, instinct, and intuition, its great guiding forces. The intellect is only ever partially involved in the works of true genius; it is more concerned with tracing their direction and meaning, laying them bare for the eyes of later observers. These laws apply above all to art—the highest and noblest of human activities, which brings it closer to its divine origin. These principles hold the same value and importance in the realm of great politics, for statesmanship, which is indeed an art, bears all the essential characteristics of artistic creativity.

The sculptor takes a chisel and hammer to raw stone to breathe divine life into it; what was once unformed marble becomes an artistic shape. The painter uses color to imitate noble forms from nature, in a certain sense, creating them anew. The poet strings together the inherently formless elements of language to create a poem, a drama, or an epic, transforming human passions—both good and evil—into profound expression.

Similarly, the statesman shapes society with the power of his will and actions, molding it into a living, breathing national body. His great, ingenious projects inspire love for his people and direct them toward shared goals. Like artists, they all draw from a reservoir of inspiration; the true artist sees himself as an instrument of this inspiration. However, in all these fields, there are also craftsmen who perform their trade with diligence and industriousness. If they are among the better in their profession, they acquire valuable, extensive knowledge, which they apply appropriately when needed. But what they do is their profession, not their calling; they are the talents of artistic activity.

In contrast, the true artist works as a genius—this is the difference between talent and genius. Talent draws from experience, knowledge, or an imaginative mind, whereas genius draws from grace. It works in pursuit of a higher mission and thus fulfills the purpose it sets out to achieve.

Visit to the Reich Chancellery (Prime Minister Gombos)

Geniuses travel worlds, determined by foresight, yes—the so-called creators of worlds and predictors of people. They set the course, even amid divisions, by maintaining their vigilance and keeping their vision from becoming clouded. The saying that there is a child hidden in every genius applies especially to these individuals, for they act and direct themselves inwardly rather than outwardly. They work out of childlike curiosity, facing challenges in the open-minded way that children often do.

The brilliant statesman achieves the possible by simplifying seemingly insurmountable challenges. While the average mind has yet to perceive the tasks awaiting a solution, the great leader is already in the process of solving them.

After the war, the most pressing task for Germans was to create a nation that thought, felt, and acted as one, drawn from a mix of states, parties, organizations, and individuals. This issue did not originate with the war, but it was this internal disunity that ultimately caused us to lose the war. For centuries, Germany was excluded from world politics due to its internal divisions. We Germans have resolved our internal differences—whether religious or social—through immense sacrifices, while other nations, who recognized their world-political destinies sooner than we did, preserved what little we still had left. But it was the war that revealed the untenable nature of our divided state. Without learning from this harsh lesson, the Germans failed to follow the clear path laid out by history.

Particularism celebrated all kinds of excesses, just as in times when we enjoyed a degree of internal freedom at the cost of external sovereignty. After the war, it often seemed as if Germany might permanently withdraw from the global stage and retreat into provincial isolation. To unify national thinking, the first and most difficult realization was that any internal struggle to restore Germany's global standing was futile from the outset and thus not worth pursuing. Germany's representatives had, after all, already secured this global standing by signing the Versailles document.

A historic encounter. Eden and Simen with the Führer

The Reich Cabinet at the Proclamation of the Military Law

Vickie Boyle & Carolynn Boyle

After the New Year's Diplomatic Reception in 1936

The Führer and Reich Minister of Foreign Affairs on Von Neurath

Meeting of Adolf Hitler with Mussolini in Venice 1934

In the Reich Canal: The Führer and his Stobach Chief Latze

The Reichskanaler at the New Year's reception in conversation with the French Ambassador Francois-Pencet

New Year's Reception 1935. The Führer speaks with the Doven of the diplomatic Corps

The Führer and the Polish Foreign Minister, Colonel Beek

And he did more by carefully monitoring adherence to the document and by perceiving every national revolt as an attack on his exile. A true statesman must not merely engage with parties of the time, nor align solely with the existing state, but rather stand outside it. The state had to dissolve to allow for a moral, political, and economic struggle that could empower the German people, creating a foundation for a genuine state aligned with their nature. In fighting against the state, it became necessary to establish a "state within the state," testing all mechanisms that would later support the new state both practically and organizationally. It was insufficient to only anticipate a new theory; a committed group was needed to bring the theory to life, giving it substance, color, and real existence.

The Boers, in opposition to the Weimar Republic, concluded in Berne that a distinct entity within the people was essential, if not an outright oppositional state, in both left and right factions. This process of forming the German nation could only be effectively challenged through such a foundation. Meanwhile, the Reich's officials at New Year's receptions and other venues required critical groundwork and forethought, serving as the actual starting point for significant political transformations. Even as an unknown private during World War I, and later amidst the revolutionary turmoil as an officer in the Bavarian garrisons, the Führer made several pivotal decisions, guided by statesmanlike confidence and an instinct for sovereign, decisive action.

On the G'schwandner Alm near Garmisch

The Führer during his summer holiday in front of the Bruckeerlehen near Berchtesgaden, where Dietrich Eckart lived for a longer period in 1923

Abend on Obersalsberg

Walks through the beech forests at sunset along the shore have often offered both education and the chance for important political decisions. During these walks, children frequently approach the guide, give him their attention, and share their small but deeply meaningful experiences. At times, the guide may even pause significant conversations to immerse himself in these moments, finding joy in the simple stories shared by the children.

In larger towns, Navy personnel gather around the Führer, enlivening short, subdued evenings with tales of war, accounts of submarine voyages, and battles such as those on the Skagerrak. The same scenes play out in small rural garrisons, where the Führer himself shares vivid and captivating stories from his experiences on the Western Front. On his journeys, he often pauses at particularly scenic spots—whether on a bright summer day or a warm, moonlit night. It is common for berry pickers and wood gatherers to come across him unexpectedly, perhaps catching him peeling an apple or slicing some bread in a forest clearing. He'll often wave over those who hesitate, inviting them to join the picnic.

Many wonder why the Führer chose Oberfalsberg as his home. But anyone who has stood there understands there is scarcely a place in Germany that offers such a sweeping, unobstructed view of natural beauty, despite the surrounding mountains. In the mountains near Horben, at the foot of the Gaisberg, sits the historic monastery town of Salzburg. On days when the Föhn winds blow, the area is filled with a distinct atmosphere. During his summer holiday near Berchtesgaden, the Führer was known to visit locations like the Bruckeriehen, where Dietrich Eckart lived for an extended time in 1923.

Pimpfe be Führer

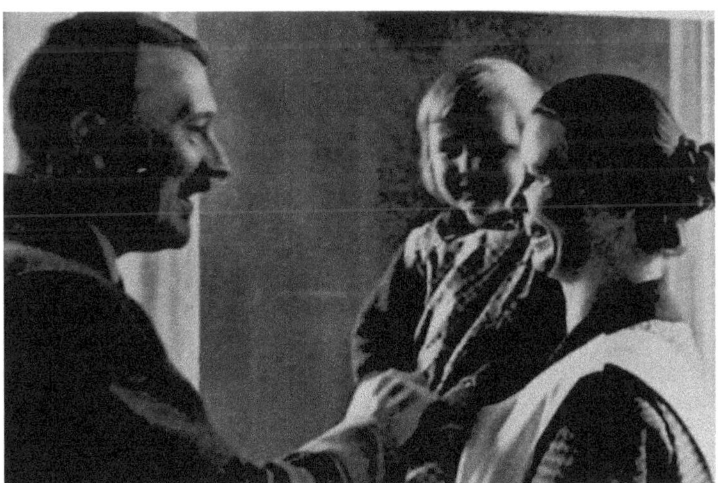

Mother's happiness

Here, My Führer, is my grandchild

The Föhn brings change to Oberer towers, revealing the massif of the Untersberg, whose shifting character transforms Oberer and Obersalzberg daily. Each day has its own mood. Sometimes, in the early morning, mist shrouds the trees, rising from the valleys to float as bright, white clouds. Other days begin with brilliant sunshine, illuminating every detail in sharp clarity. Warm winds descend, filling the valleys with towering snowstorms that lash the mountains, while fierce winds roar around the modest country house.

It is here, in this magnificent natural setting—a mirror to the course of human events—that the Führer resides while preparing his great speeches, which have often inspired new directions not only within Germany but in world politics. In this place, decisive discussions shape the laws whose impacts will last for centuries. A German-American from the Steuben Society once fully grasped the significance of this humble country house during a visit to his homeland. Reflecting on the experience, he later remarked, "Here, I feel the presence of generations—here is my legacy for my grandchild."

The Führer in front of his country house on Oberfalsberg

We did not truly know Germany. We only knew the Germany of old, and we saw it again in the new Germany when we visited the palaces and castles of earlier times. But with the Führer gone, a deep calm settles over the land; these are his hours of peace.

However, the next morning, the phone exchange reports dozens of calls. By now, we have come to understand this house and experienced firsthand the contrast between the Germany created by Adolf Hitler and the old order. We also now understand the boundless resources from which he draws inspiration. It is true that here, far from the chaos of daily life, his mind—guided by the unshakable grandeur of the landscape—finds direction for the people and the fatherland.

But the Führer cannot enjoy this wonderful natural beauty like a traveler who has left his work behind. As soon as he arrives at the Obersalzberg, he faces a mountain of letters, documents, telegrams, and calls, with new work arriving daily. Almost every day, ministers and Reich leaders seek his opinion on important matters. Sometimes, they travel to Berchtesgaden themselves, needing his counsel even during his brief moments of rest.

Here, issues of the party that had to be put aside for more urgent decisions in Berlin are addressed. Books, both literary and political, from home and abroad—left unread at the Reich Chancellery—are reviewed here in peace. Often, the light in his room remains on late into the night as he works, long after his companions have gone to sleep.

Even on "recreation" at Obersalzberg, the post office and telephone exchange in Berchtesgaden are busy. The Führer's entourage, too, has its hands full as ideas emerge and decisions take shape swiftly. Before breakfast, he reviews the newspapers, reading edited clippings himself. His adjutants, press officer, and other associates provide a brief report of the day's agenda. After breakfast, registered visitors—Reich leaders, ministers, close colleagues, and party members—arrive.

Mail is then presented to the Führer, who provides quick responses or dictates them directly. The morning passes quickly, and his old comrades are frequent visitors to the Obersalzberg. Among them are Goring, Dr. Goebbels, Reich Treasurer Schwarz, Minister Adolf Wagner, the Reich War Minister, and others. After a busy morning, there's usually a short or long stroll or a trip to nearby areas. The Führer particularly enjoys hikes to the "Goll-Häusl" in both winter and summer.

At the Obersee near Berchtesgaden

During the summer holiday on the Oberfalsberg

Dismissed from his duties, he departed from Danzig, from Saxony—if only for a break from his work—to join the Führer and discuss plans. The Führer, in high spirits, spends his time in the garden, a place both calming and inspiring for him. The veterans of the previous war are always welcomed guests, sharing stories under clear skies or in the crunch of winter snow.

In the big city, the guide moves swiftly and effortlessly, carrying with him the thoughts and wishes of the people, whose fervent hopes remain unspoken yet deeply felt. Jubilant cheers break out when he appears, and workers from all around—those from the factories and others across the land—gather to catch a glimpse of him. Many have traveled far to express their admiration, and their greetings resound as they shout unexpectedly, moved by the occasion.

One thing is certain: nowhere else does the guide encounter such a life so suited to his character and to the diverse German regions represented. From Upper Silesia, East Prussia, Schleswig, and beyond, thousands come together, knowing that the work begun here will continue to live on in his people for millennia.

Chapter 4

The Leader as a Statesman

By

Dr. Joseph Goebbels

Human greatness has its origins in blood. Instinct is your guide, and intuition is your great grace. The mind is always only partially involved in the works of true genius; it is more concerned with tracing their direction and meaning and exposing them to the eye of the latcr observer. These laws apply above all to art, the highest and noblest human activity, which brings it closer to its divine origin. They hold equal value and significance in the field of major politics, which we do not call statecraft for anything. Statecraft is, in fact, an art, as it possesses all the essential characteristics of artistic creativity.

The sculptor sets a chisel and hammer into the unformed stone to breathe divine spirit into it: what was raw marble becomes artistic form. The painter uses the material of color to recreate nature's noble creations and, to a certain extent, to shape them a second time. The poet transforms the inherently formless language into a poem, a drama, or an epic depiction, through which he conveys the human passions of good and evil.

The statesman, meanwhile, has the raw material of the masses at his disposal. With the power of his word and work, he kneads them into a living and breathing national body: his great, ingenious projects present the people with the nation's ultimate goals. All of them draw uniformly from the vision of genius, which is essentially an inspiration—the true artist's innate instrument.

In each of these fields, there are also craftsmen who operate within the boundaries of their tasks and duties. They learn their trade through hard work and dedication, and if they are among the best in their profession, they acquire valuable and extensive specialist knowledge, which they can use as needed. But what they do is a job, not a calling. They are the talents of artistic activity.

The true artist, however, appears as a genius. This is where talent differs from genius: talent draws from experience, knowledge, and perhaps also an imaginative mind, while genius draws from grace. It executes a higher order and fulfills the position in which it participates.

New Year's reception of the diplomatic corps 1934

Visit to the Reich Chancellery (Prime Minister Gombos)

Senies overthrow worlds and build new ones. They are the great guides of people; times are aligned with them. They set the course of history. The saying that "there is a man" applies above all to the child hidden in every genius, for he acts and works from a childlike intuition and faces things with the self-assured awareness with which children tend to approach life. The brilliant statesman dares the impossible in order to make the possible achievable. His real strength lies in simplifying seemingly insoluble relationships. Before the average mind has even seen or recognized the tasks that await solutions, the great leader is already in the process of solving them.

The most urgent problem for us Germans after the war was to form a nation that thought, felt, and acted as one, unifying the conglomerate of states, parties, organizations, and individuals. The war did not first create this problem, but its unresolved nature ultimately caused us to lose it. For many centuries, Germany was excluded from global political action due to internal divisions. We Germans have resolved internal differences of opinion—whether religious, economic, or social—at great cost, while other nations, having recognized their global destinies sooner, took possession of the world.

The war made the unsustainability of this situation clear. Rather than learning from this terrible lesson, the Germans did the opposite of what history required of them. In Germany, particularism celebrated countless orgies, just as it had in times when we most needed unity. In the years after the war, it sometimes seemed as though Germany was about to permanently withdraw from the world stage, retreating into provincial isolation. The need to unify national thinking was evident; yet, the so-called Weimar Constitution represented, in some ways, a perpetuation of internal discord, with parliamentary parties serving as focal points of division.

The state avoided this essential task, directing its attention more inward than outward. Its goal became the preservation of what little internal freedom and external sovereignty we still possessed. For a statesman with true genius, the first and most difficult realization was to recognize that any struggle within the state itself to restore Germany's global standing was futile from the start. The state had forfeited this standing once and for all by having its representatives sign the Versailles Treaty.

The fact that, at the time, they were understood by almost no one but later became the true cause of tremendous and fateful consequences confirms the correctness of the worldview reflected in his actions. It would have been easy for him to join one of the established parties. Opportunities for advancement beckoned him there. He could have soothed his troubled conscience by accepting that what currently existed had to be preserved, and thus, it seemed necessary to choose the lesser evil. He did none of that. He did not do so because none of the existing parties offered any guarantee or even the possibility of overcoming the internal German division, and without the unification of the Germans, a solution to the national German problem in a statesmanlike sense was ruled out from the outset. Here, we already see the instinctive insight of a gifted man who would rather face the seemingly hopeless struggle of challenging the state, money, press, and parties from nothing rather than compromise at the outset of his work.

Reich Press Chief Dr. Dietrich submits press reports to the Führer. At that time, it was fashionable to go along with the state. Two reasons were commonly given for this: one identified with the state, while the other believed it should and could be reformed from within. The Führer took neither of these into consideration, as he knew this state was flawed at its core, that it could not be restructured, and that it had to be abolished to make way for the formation of a true state. Later, there were people and parties who, once they had recognized (or pretended to have recognized) the impossibility of reforming the Weimar system from within, opposed it from the outside; but they were not truly in alignment with the Führer.

Reich Press Chief Dr. Dietrich submits press reports to the Fuhrer

In the Reich Chancellery

English Front-line soldiers with the Fuhrer

Remembrance Day 1934. The celebration at the Berlin State Opera

Burdened from the outset with the compromise of a peace agreement—albeit a temporary one—with the Weimar democracy, only the Führer could claim, from the first to the last day of his opposition, that he had never made a pact with the parliamentary regime. This lack of compromise seemed to mark him as the only one destined to deliver the final blow at the last hour.

People did not appeal to either the educated classes or the proletariat. Instead, they had the courage to express all the unpopular truths and refused to buy the approval of the masses with cheap flattery. Today, we must return to these origins of the National Socialist movement and of Adolf Hitler's genuine leadership in order to comprehend the miracle of his statesmanship, which is already evident in these early beginnings. For it was not time that changed the leader, but the leader who changed the times. What once seemed paradoxical has now long become self-evident. This transformation required a clear and uncompromising decision by one man, along with a tough and relentless struggle, before it was accepted.

It would have been easy at the time to make extravagant social demands, especially when the leader and his movement were far from being in a position to fulfill their promises. It is also fair to admit that, during those first few years, recruiting supporters in this way might have been convenient. However, the leader did not take this path. Instead, he created an ideological foundation for his movement, which became, in a sense, the supporting structure of his party and state. The most significant aspect of this ideology was the connection between national and socialist principles, which, in a straightforward manner understandable even to the common man, reconciled the real driving forces of the time—forces that had been in bitter conflict.

The fact that nothing needed to be changed in the program, the worldview, the flag, or the name of the National Socialist movement when it came to power is proof of the foresight and statesmanship with which the party's foundations were laid, even in its early days. Under the Führer's guidance, the party was trained to make no compromises, combining the strictest principles with great flexibility in its methods. From its very inception, it waged a life-and-death struggle against parliamentarian.

Remembrance Day 1934: The celebration at the Berlin State Opera marked a time when political parties and leaders rarely addressed the people as a unified whole. Instead, they spoke only to separate segments of the population. The workers' parties spoke to workers, the bourgeois parties to citizens, the religious parties to congregations, and the farmers' parties to farmers. At the early meetings of the National Socialist Workers' Party in Munich, when the leader could barely gather a hundred people, it may have seemed grotesque to a superficial observer that he nevertheless always addressed the people as a unified entity.

The Fuhrer in front of the Goslar Imperial Palace on Thanksgiving Day, 1934

Parties do not rely on lazy and cowardly phrases but rather counter brute force with brute force. If their bold initial attempt to seize power on November 8–9, 1923, failed, later historians will need to examine not only what was achieved but also what was prevented. Already, one can say that their judgment will ultimately vindicate the Führer's actions.

How did bourgeois politicians behave after losing attempted coups in the days of the Republic? They either fled abroad or claimed they were not involved. The Führer, however, was different. He stood by his team, was the first among the accused, and did not take advantage of any escape route offered by the court or government. He openly admitted that he had attempted to overthrow the state and declared that he would do it again if given the opportunity. In doing what was evidently the most dangerous and destructive act possible at that moment, he preserved the movement and his work.

His conduct during the major trial before the Munich People's Court was a statesmanlike act of the highest order, displaying every element of political action in the best sense. Boldness was paired with logic, openness with courage, and contempt for danger with unwavering determination. It was a high-stakes game in which everything was won because everything was risked. This self-defense against the monstrous state of Versailles and Weimar became a higher moral principle, and hundreds of thousands, even millions, who had only dreamed or longed for this vision, joined in a wave of enthusiastic admiration.

The Führer's refusal to seek agreements with superficially similar parties within parliamentary life, choosing instead to re-found the movement on the same core principles, demonstrates how clearly he recognized the statesmanlike tasks that awaited him and his followers after his release. The re-establishment of the party was a long, difficult, and costly struggle. For years, the endeavor appeared hopeless. During this period, the NSDAP wasn't even deemed worthy of hatred by its opponents. Yet what may have seemed insignificant externally was, internally, a fertile and organic process of gradual reconstruction of the movement and its individual organizations.

The Führer in front of the Goslar Imperial Palace on Thanksgiving Day 1934: If a leader wants to gather around himself individuals of intelligence, character, and strong temperament, he need not fear judgment for doing so. Rarely has an era witnessed such a wealth of genuine experts as ours. Today, it's easy to see that they exist, but it was far more challenging to identify them among the broad masses of followers, to recognize their talents instinctively, and to assign them roles within the movement and later within the state that suited their abilities.

The Foreign Military attaches at the Party Congress at Nuremberg

In 1928, only 12 representatives of the National Socialist movement entered parliament. However, this number grew almost tenfold within two years, exposing the party to the public and presenting it with a decisive test. Like previous parties, it could have settled for a few token ministerial positions and participated in the existing regime, but it also had the option to pursue its fight to the end under the slogan: "All or nothing!" The Führer's instinct as a statesman once again led to the right decision, choosing to continue the battle unwaveringly.

He understood that enforcing the principle of legality against extremists within his own ranks was essential for the movement's success. His next goal was to systematically undermine the bourgeois parties. After two years of relentless effort, the Brüning cabinet was brought down. The National Socialist movement's apparent tolerance toward the Papen government ultimately led to the critical moment on August 13, 1932—a moment that would test true statesmanship.

During the Reichswehr trial before the Leipzig State Court, the Führer proclaimed the principle of legality, a strategy that ultimately shifted the outcome in his favor. At the beginning of this trial, few in the regime suspected its eventual impact, but by its end, a Berlin Democratic newspaper acknowledged Adolf Hitler as the trial's real victor. The highest German court had effectively provided him with a public platform to affirm his stance on legality, which he could now reference in his continued opposition to the Republic. This point marked a turning point and underscored the Führer's difference from his opponents, as he saw the strategic possibilities of this trial from the outset rather than recognizing them only in hindsight.

Faced with the choice of settling for partial satisfaction or striving for total victory, the Führer chose the latter. Unlike countless political figures in Germany's past who would have accepted a compromise, he pursued an all-or-nothing approach. This bold decision cost him two million votes in the November 1932 election, yet he pressed on with renewed intensity in the Lippe election campaign in January 1933. Within two weeks, he ascended to power.

The alliance between Hindenburg and Hitler symbolized a new era of reconstruction, merging tradition with revolution. The Führer's statesmanlike skill achieved the extraordinary feat of a peaceful revolution of unprecedented scale, aligning revolutionary change with traditional forces and avoiding significant bloodshed.

A meeting of the Reich Chancellery under the chairmanship of the Fuhrer

The Fuhrer received a Japanese naval delegation in 1934

This success was the result of an unmistakable sense of what was feasible and what was not at that moment. It stemmed from a clarity of vision paired with decisive action. It arose from an unspoiled political instinct capable of extraordinary feats, driven by a belief in the extraordinary. Today, Germany is home to a transformed people, a nation that, compared to a decade ago, now draws strength and faith from the resolute leadership of a true statesman—a leader who not only knows what he seeks but is wholly committed to it.

He stands among the select few in history, demonstrating a greatness born from simplicity and a simplicity that reflects true greatness.

On May 1st, on the Templhofer Feld

The Führer, alongside the Reich Minister of War and the Commander-in-Chief of the Army, during the 1935 maneuvers at the Munsterlager military training area.

Bombers over Nuremberg

First inspection of the Richthofen Squadron

German troops over the Mainz Rhine Bridge on March 7, 1936

The new tank weapon

When the Führer's decision on October 14, 1932, to withdraw from the League of Nations became known, almost all of Germany welcomed it with joy, as it was widely seen as a first step toward restoring Germany's freedom in defense. Since that memorable day in Potsdam, the German army has marched alongside party formations on national holidays. This new army represents a true "people's army" that does not distinguish based on origin, wealth, or social status, much like the party itself. It stands shoulder to shoulder with the people, whether on festive or solemn occasions—be it May 1st, Thanksgiving Day, or the annual rally in Nuremberg.

In his significant address to the Reichstag on January 30, 1934, marking the anniversary of the National Socialist Revolution, he spoke of the bond between the Wehrmacht and the people. He described a unique historical relationship, where a warm alliance had formed between the revolutionary forces and the disciplined leadership of the Wehrmacht, symbolized by the partnership between the National Socialist Party and himself as a leader, along with the officers and soldiers of the German Reich Army and Navy.

Every recruit in the armed forces, wearing the insignia of the National Socialist movement on his uniform, reflects the close relationship between the Party and the Wehrmacht. The Führer, together with Hindenburg, frequently emphasized that the Party and the Wehrmacht are the two pillars on which the structure of the National Socialist Third Reich rests. He asserted firmly that while the Party embodies the political will, the Wehrmacht carries the nation's weaponry. Out of conscious and voluntary resolve, the Wehrmacht has merged into the new state in a thoroughly National Socialist spirit, allying itself fully for better or for worse.

This connection is evident in various gestures: from the introduction of the comradely salute in the National Socialist branches, participation in all Party and state celebrations, to the adoption of the Party's emblem in the Wehrmacht, involvement in Party congresses, and the hoisting of the war flag adorned with the swastika. The duties of the German soldier are infused with a nationalist ethos, as seen in the oath of allegiance, which pledges service to the Führer with unwavering loyalty to the new state.

The Wehrmacht, therefore, does not operate as an independent entity but as a National Socialist force within a National Socialist state. This is proudly evident in its outward symbols, with every member, from the rank-and-file to the Commander-in-Chief, aligned under this unified ideology.

Day of the Wehrmacht Nuremberg 1935: Motorized heavy artillery

We have tanks again through Hitler's act

The Greyhounds of the Baltic Sea: A German Speedboat

Fleet visit to Kiel in 1934

Vickie Boyle & Carolynn Boyle

Visit to the Landsberg Fortress in 1934

The formation of the National Socialist formation on November 9, 1935, on the almost completed Konigsplats

Motor-SA in front of the Führer at the Reich Party Congress in 1935

Photo taken during his imprisonment in 1924 at Landsberg Fortress

Visit of the Führer after 10 years. At the window of his cell

At a conference during the fighting. A speaker speaks, and the Führer takes short notes. From left to right 1st row: Heb, Rust, the Fuhrer, Zorner, Kerl

2nd row: Behind Heb Schreckt

About The Author

Took fifty years to complete my literary life's work. 1975 when it all started. I wanted to be a paper back writer.

Vickie Boyle

Cambridge senior high school graduate 2024.

Co-Author: Carolynn Boyle